AGILE METHODOLOGY FOR
DEVELOPING & MEASURING LEARNING

AGILE METHODOLOGY FOR DEVELOPING & MEASURING LEARNING

TRAINING DEVELOPMENT
FOR
TODAY'S WORLD

Kaliym A. Islam, M.Ed.

authorHOUSE®

AuthorHouse™ *LLC*
1663 Liberty Drive
Bloomington, IN 47403
www.authorhouse.com
Phone: 1-800-839-8640

Published by AuthorHouse   10/23/2013

ISBN: 978-1-4918-2383-5 (sc)
ISBN: 978-1-4918-2388-0 (e)

Library of Congress Control Number: 2013918068

CONTENTS

CHAPTER FIVE

SECTION TWO

CHAPTER SIX

CHAPTER SEVEN

CHAPTER EIGHT

CHAPTER NINE

SECTION THREE

ABOUT THIS BOOK

Why is this topic important?

Technologies of the last five years have drastically changed and reshaped how we live and learn. The net of these changes, according to the Boston Consulting Group, is that consumers are reacting faster and demanding more. They now expect instant access to information, frequent updates, and flawless performance—and not just inside the space of technology itself—but also the products they interact with. To keep up with consumer expectations, the most successful companies have learned to change the way they do business. They've adopted product development approaches that shorten the lifecycle, thereby allowing these businesses to supplement their major product launches with frequent, iterative updates.

This abbreviated, incremental approach to product development is forcing training organizations to rethink how they develop future learning solutions that support said business systems. Traditional training development methodologies such as Instructional System Design (ISD) typically result in increased administrative overhead, long development lifecycles, and large learning solutions that are rarely updated. Agile, however, provides training developers with the opportunity to minimize paperwork, shorten development timelines, and provide frequent, timely updates to learning solutions.

Businesses that employ the Agile approach to product development are experiencing increased customer satisfaction, highly engaged employees, greater visibility into the process of product releases, improved ability to address changes, and even higher quality products. And now, training organizations that employ Agile can realize these same benefits.

What can you achieve with this book?

This book can help transform your training development methodology into one that allows you to rapidly respond to ever-changing business needs. It will teach you how to deliver learning solutions that are both timely and effective. It will introduce you to a flexible development technique, one that allows you to keep pace with fast-changing business conditions. It will show you how to achieve better collaboration with your business partners. It will help you create empowered, self-organizing, cross-functional teams that can distill large training efforts into smaller components, which can then be developed and delivered over multiple iterations. Finally, this book will help you assess if the organizational structure of your training department is currently optimized to support the needs of your company.

How is this book organized?

This book is organized into three sections. Section One provides a background of the Agile methodology. It gives a brief history of this unique approach to development and makes the case for why learning organizations should adapt this technique. Section Two walks you through the Agile methodology as applied to training and development, providing a step-by-step approach to implementation. Section Three is a case study on how the customer training organization of the Depository Trust & Clearing Corporation (DTCC) successfully implemented the Agile method as their approach to training development.

To my sons Taariq, Kaliym, Isaiah, and Khary

PREFACE

In October 2007 I co-authored an article for Training Industry Inc. titled "The Training Value Gap." My thesis was that delivering small nuggets of learning incrementally rather than waiting until the entire learning program was complete, allowed learners to quickly absorb at least some of the required knowledge and skills, and, as a result, rapidly translate those skills into incremental performance improvements. This, in turn, helps the organization reap the benefits of its employees' improved knowledge and skill-sets much earlier than if it would have delayed training.

When Bobbi Edwards and I wrote that article seven years ago, we had never heard of Agile. Even though we had our own theory regarding a new approach to designing learning solutions, we didn't (as yet) have a methodology to support it. Over the years, my teams had attempted to accomplish this fresh approach to learning solutions through a variety of waterfall development approaches, including Six Sigma. It wasn't until the organizations that I managed began using Agile that we realized: what if we leveraged this iterative, incremental approach to learning program design, development, and deployment—all in a sustained, proactive manner?

For those not familiar with Agile and how this approach to product development has changed our everyday lives, consider how you currently receive updates to your smartphone apps or your personal computer software. Chances are you frequently receive small functionality updates to these applications, right? It's a stark contrast to the mindset of just a few years ago when software applications underwent major rewrites every eighteen to twenty-four months. Delivering incremental software fixes and functionality now allows customers to receive value faster and more frequently (as opposed to waiting up to two years for all of the desired functionalities to be built into a new release!).

Consider the impact to today's customers if they had to wait two years to tweet the contents of a web page simply because the company that built the browser had delayed updates until they could also build a code that allowed users to post to Facebook and Google+. Agile not only provides software developers with a methodology that supports incremental releases, it also accommodates for the quick and nimble change of the high-tech world in which we live. As a result, we all glean the benefits of frequent fixes and increased functionality.

Applying this analogy to training allows the new manager, who needs to quickly develop leadership skills, the ability to master the skill of chairing a meeting even if the component of the curriculum that teaches how to navigate the company's culture hasn't yet been built. The implications are: this new manager (and his or her company) can immediately benefit from one component of the training even though the entire learning program isn't finished. This allows the company to receive incremental value from the training, therefore, reducing the training value gap. When training content is developed and delivered the Agile way, companies and trainees can both realize the benefit of learning solutions sooner, not later.

If you want to close the training value gap, I encourage you to use Agile.

Kaliym A. Islam

ACKNOWLEDGMENTS

I want to thank the following individuals for helping to make this book a reality: First and foremost my editor, CJ Schepers, for helping me find my voice, and Earl Gamble for providing sharp, insightful feedback. Many thanks also to Barbara Edwards, Marcus Smith, and Roger Roess for being willing to take chances as a great leadership team. Finally, gratitude to the best Agile learning team on the planet one could hope for, specifically Valtina Sylvain, Michael Berry, Louay Kaddah, Jafar Miah, Kristen Hancox, Cheryl Zak, Sharri-Lynn Goldstein, David Wong, Bill Corrigan, James Gilchrist, Joe Wheeler, Tony Leone, and Jason Sackel, and last but never least, Kiersten Yocum.

I couldn't have done this without all of you challenging me and cheering me on.

INTRODUCTION

The businesses that training organizations support have changed. Influences like social media, speedier times to market, and customer demand for getting things quicker have transformed the way businesses get things done. Take the food industry, for example. Research commissioned by allfoodbusiness.com found that social media has overtaken traditional marketing outlets, and that food customers are demanding faster service and quicker response times. The Boston Consulting Group (BCG) recently conducted a study that supports the allfoodbusiness.com report. Moreover, BCG found that consumers, in all industries, now "react faster and are more demanding," in general.

> "They expect instant access to information, frequent updates, and flawless performance not just in the technology space, but with every product that they interact with."
>
> —The Boston Consulting Group (BCG)

So, if this is a reality for business, then it must also be a reality for the training organizations that support those businesses.

Corporate IT departments were ahead of the curve in understanding the importance of using a development approach that mirrored the needs of the business they served. This realization resulted in IT moving away from some of the software development techniques that might have worked just a decade ago, and leaning toward the use of more lightweight or agile approaches.

This shift has been rapid when you consider that in the year 2000 the use of Agile in software development was only about 1 percent. By 2011, Agile usage had increased in the software development world by 60 to 80 percent. This migration has allowed IT departments to keep up with the pace of business and its achievements in a number of areas.

If training organizations follow the path of their IT colleagues, they too, can realize improvements that include:

- Improved quality

- More opportunities for mid-course correction

- Improved satisfaction

- Better business alignment

- Improved time to market

All of this backstory leads us to the if/then statement for training professionals that I learned many years ago as an engineering major trying to program computers. If businesses need to increase their speed to market and quickly respond to changing customer requirements, then the training departments that support those businesses must also do the same. One smart approach is to adopt Agile as a training development methodology.

Now, for those training professionals who've either heard that Agile is difficult or whom all things IT intimidates, there's no need to fear. This program does not require anyone to be a techie or learn a brand-new vocabulary. It's not a ScrumMaster® certification program (you'll learn a little later exactly what a ScrumMaster is).

The Agile way doesn't consist of complicated statistical tools that may not apply to what you do, and it doesn't ask you to forget everything you've ever learned about instructional design, training, and development.

This book will do the following:

- Introduce you to the concepts of Agile;

- Expose you to Agile tools to use right away;

- Introduce you to a proven methodology that can be easily implemented; and

- Allow you and your organization to immediately realize the benefit of using Agile for training and development.

So, the objective here is to help you use Agile as a training and development methodology. The major topics that we'll cover are:

- What is Agile?

- The Agile process

- How to use Agile for T+D

Now that we have a good understanding of what this book and course is all about as well as why it's important, let's dig our heels in and get started. I'll see you in the next section.

SECTION ONE
An Introduction to Agile

Welcome to Section One of *Agile Methodology for Developing & Measuring Learning*. It will provide you with a basic background and general understanding of Agile development.

Once you've completed this section, you'll have a good understanding of Agile and, as a result, be able to explain just why trainers should use Agile development. You'll also be able to explain the importance of the Agile Manifesto and principles. Most importantly, as a training professional, you'll be able to explain the differences between various approaches to Agile. This will help you to decide which version of Agile to use in your organization.

I'm really excited for you and wish you good luck in your journey. So let's get started!

CHAPTER ONE
What Is Agile?

Here is where your journey into Agile begins. This chapter will provide you with the background you'll need in order to understand what we'll be teaching you later. It will help you better understand Agile, by providing you with a good working definition of the process. When you complete this section, you'll also be able to identify the attributes of the Agile methodology and the historic events that allowed it to evolve into what it is today.

So, what exactly is Agile?

Kent Beck, one of the founders of Agile software development, describes Agile as a group of software development methods based on iterative and incremental development where requirements and solutions evolve through collaboration between self-organizing, cross-functional teams. (OK, not exactly a short definition.) He goes on to point out that Agile supports flexibility and rapid response to change.[1] And, software engineer Craig Larman refers to Agile as iterative development.[2] In short, Agile is a development approach that supports flexibility and rapid response to change.

Agile promotes adaptive planning, meaning that the plan you start with might not end up being the approach you use to complete the project. Agile also promotes evolutionary development and delivery. This means that what you "thought" you were going to build may not be what you ultimately build. Finally, Agile promotes a time-boxed iterative approach to product development, and

---

[1]   http://agile.dzone.com/news/interview-kent-beck-circa-2001

[2]   http://www.youtube.com/watch?v=Wbk1zDTHp4E

encourages rapid and flexible responses to change. So in summary, a good working definition of Agile is this:

"Agile is a development approach that supports flexibility and rapid response to change."

Unlike traditional approaches to software development whereby huge amounts of analysis and documentation must be completed before a project begins, Agile uses the least amount of documentation necessary to quickly deliver a high-quality project. This doesn't mean Agile forgoes required documentation; however, the goal is to keep the documentation to a minimum and not burden the team.

In Agile, any planning at the project's start is kept to a minimum, yet the planning process continues throughout the entire project lifecycle, and involves the entire team of Customers, Developers, Quality Assurance Technicians, and Analysts.

Another difference between Agile and other development approaches is that changes can be made throughout the life of the project with little ceremony. In other words, individuals can request changes to their requirements at anytime without having to endure a long, arduous change management process.

This is in direct contrast to other approaches that require customers to endure formal and time-consuming "change management" documentation just to tweak one requirement. With Agile, customers can get new requirements integrated into their products at a late-stage release. This feature is endearing to many stakeholders who work with Agile teams.

To understand the potential implications of Agile in the world of training and development, consider the experience that many instructional designers have endured when attempting to develop a large training program:

After spending months gaining an understanding of the training needs and audience profile, writing instructional objectives, and getting approval of the course outline, conditions suddenly change or a new subject matter expert (SME) is introduced into the project. The new SME now wants to change the objectives and has issues with the outline. A change request is filed, the objectives are updated, and the new outline is approved. A business emergency then occurs, and the SME isn't available for several weeks. When the SME finally has time to review whatever the designer has created, the expert has a different take on what needs to be developed. Again, another change process is required. Except this time, during the review process, it's discovered that the business system the training was built to support has also changed and now two of the six modules need their screen shots adjusted. Once this is completed, however, the SME decides to reword information in the previously approved components of the other modules. Six months to a year later, there's still been no training content for students who urgently need it.

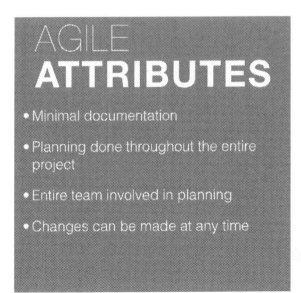

AGILE
ATTRIBUTES

- Minimal documentation

- Planning done throughout the entire project

- Entire team involved in planning

- Changes can be made at any time

Agile allows for the quick development and deployment of the most critical training components so that even if the entire program isn't deployed, students still benefit from micro lessons. It also provides a mechanism for adapting to the inevitable changes of any development project.

With Agile, developers are never locked into a linear course of action to define, design, develop, and then test the entire software product prior to delivery. Instead, the Agile approach allows developers to deliver smaller components or functionality of the larger deliverable via frequent and small iterations, while requirements for the larger deliverable can be developed over multiple iterations.

Mobile application updates are just one example of Agile development in practice. In today's world, small pieces of functionality or updates are delivered to your device(s) on an iterative, frequent basis. This is different from the "old days" when you had to wait nearly two years for a software package rewrite.

So, where exactly did this approach come from? What's the history of Agile?

The History of Agile

Most experts believe that the Agile methodology has its roots in IBM and the incremental software development movement of 1957. Some, however, attribute it to the adaptive software development process championed by E.A. Edmonds in 1974. Others credit Dan Gielan and the New York Telephone Company's Systems Development Center as forerunners to Agile. These iterative approaches to software development continued to evolve through the mid-1990s as an alternative to the heavyweight waterfall-oriented techniques.

Waterfall development is a process that requires one phase or component be completed and signed off on before the next phase begins. In training, this is a hindrance because we can't start designing a learning program until analysis is complete. The founders of Agile felt that waterfall techniques were too regulated, too regimented, and overly micromanaged.

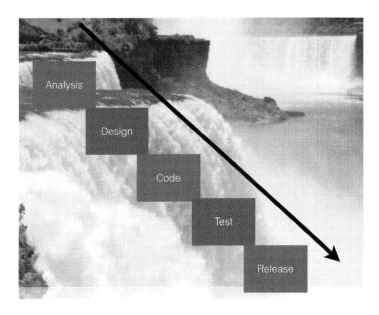

They believed that using waterfall approaches such as this contributed to a company's failure to meet the "real" customer requirements. It also caused delays getting their product to market and resulted in delivery of low-quality products that were misaligned with the business strategy.

Do these challenges sound familiar? How often have you gotten requirements at the beginning of a project and then proceeded to build a solution . . . only to find out later that the requirements have changed?

Waterfall	Agile
Failure to meet the "real" requirements	Ability to create and respond to change
Delays in time to market	Ability to balance stability and flexibility
Low quality	Ability to deliver quickly
Lack of alignment to business strategy	

The founders of Agile saw that lightweight iterative approaches would increase their capacity to quickly respond to change, create a balance between stability and flexibility of the products they were developing, and allow faster delivery. In practice, most of us today receive the benefits of Agile development and incremental updates almost daily. Until now, we just didn't know that Agile was behind the results.

Take a look at your smartphone, tablet, or other mobile device. Have you had an update to one of your apps in the past week? Chances are, yes. In fact, you've probably received a number of them. This frequent delivery of small, incremental updates is Agile—at work.

While we might not have previously known that the process used to deliver these solutions was based on Agile, we now know differently.

Incremental Updates

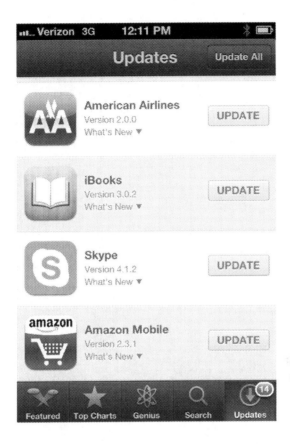

Chapter 1 Summary

So let's do a quick review of what we've covered in this section. First, we provided a working definition of Agile. We also identified some of the Agile methodology attributes as well as the historic events that allowed it to evolve. Finally, we took a look at an everyday example (our mobile devices) of how Agile is used today.

In the next chapter, we'll learn just a few of the reasons why trainers should use the Agile approach to develop their programs.

CHAPTER TWO

Why Trainers Should Use Agile

In the previous chapter we spoke about why Agile for training departments is so important. In this chapter, we'll provide more rationale for why training departments should adopt the Agile methodology and make the case for why training professionals should turn to Agile as a development approach. We'll also look at some additional challenges facing today's training organizations. We'll examine the current approaches to developing training programs and discuss their shortcomings by comparing them to the software development methodologies that they mimic. Finally, we'll explore another, less effective attempt to introduce an iterative approach to training development.

Let's start by looking at some of the challenges facing today's training organizations.

What Are the Problems Facing Today's Trainers?

Perhaps the biggest challenge trainers face today is this: practitioners don't believe their processes are as effective as they could be. Surveys conducted by the American Society for Training and Development (ASTD), the standard bearer of the vocation, suggest that course designers themselves feel that the current approaches they're using must "adapt" in order to support changing environments and take advantage of new technologies.

Dr. Gary P. Hamel, the American management expert rated by *The Wall Street Journal* as one of the world's most influential business thinkers, refers to the ASTD survey to point out the necessity for training professionals to rely on innovative methodologies that adapt as fast as the businesses that they support demand it.[3]

Another study of learning professionals, this one conducted by CERTPOINT Learning, uncovered that training professionals themselves believe current learning development methodologies cannot keep pace with the speed of change in the organizations they support. Clearly, there are a number of specific challenges facing training organizations today, including:

- A lack of confidence on the part of practitioners;

- The failure to consistently meet the real-time customer requirements;

- Delays in time to market;

---

[3] http://www.astd.org/Publications/Magazines/TD/TD-Archive/2012/08/ Long-View-Gary-Hamel

- Low quality; and

- Lack of alignment with the business strategy.

These were the same challenges facing software developers more than a decade ago. So, what methodologies are training professionals currently using to develop these programs? Everyone reading this book knows that the primary approach to training design has been instructional systems design (ISD).

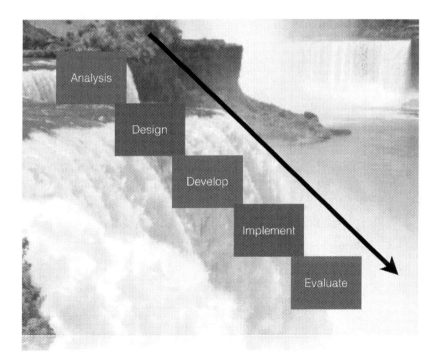

ISD is a waterfall approach to training development and modeled after popular software development methodologies. The process starts with an analysis, which then results in the creation of an outline and objectives. This outline typically requires approval before the next phase of the process (design) begins.

The result of the design phase is a design document or storyboard that must also be approved before development begins. The final solution must also get approval and sign off before the implementation and evaluation phases launch.

At every step in the process there's a review and approval requirement, which typically results in changed requirements, reworks, and delays in getting the training solution to market. If you compare the past challenges of the software development industry (which led them to use Agile) with the challenges facing training development today, you'll find unsettling similarities. Check out the chart below:

Challenges	Software Development	Training Development
Failure to meet the "real" requirements	✓	✓
Delays in time to market	✓	✓
Low quality	✓	✓
Lack of alignment to business strategy	✓	✓

So the approaches to software development that existed years ago and the current popular approach to training development are both challenged with a failure to meet the real requirements of business, delays in getting product to market, delivery of a low-quality product, and a lack of alignment to the company and its business strategy. That's why today's trainer must find a way to overcome the same challenges that once plagued software developers.

One Attempt at Iterative Training Development

There have been attempts by at least one innovator to make the training and development process more iterative. Dr. Michael W. Allen, chairman and CEO of Allen Interactions, pioneered the SAVVY™ approach in the late nineties, and recently updated that process with something he calls SAM® (Successive Approximation Model), a type of Agile development model.

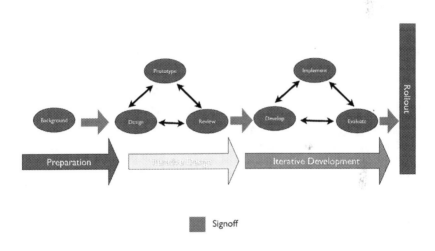

Dr. Allen's approach calls for a three-pronged process to training development: a background phase where requirements are gathered; an iterative design phase where agreement is reached regarding what should be included in the learning solution and how it should look; and finally, an iterative development phase where the learning solution is constructed.

What we find when we examine this approach, however, is that while it's indeed iterative, the process is essentially a mini-waterfall one. Yes, iteration exists inside both the design and development phases, but nothing moves into the development phase until the current design phase is approved. While Dr. Allen's approach is a significant improvement to the ISD model, it falls short of Agile's lightweight framework and flexibility.

Chapter 2 Summary

So let's do a quick review of what we covered in this chapter. We discussed some of the challenges facing training organizations today, which included educating practitioners that their current processes aren't as effective as they could be, why they need more innovation, and the importance of keeping pace with the businesses they support.

We looked at ISD, the current development methodology most training organizations use, and found that it's similar to the heavyweight software development approaches of the past, which is why we made the move to Agile in the first place. We also looked at one other approach to training development, Dr. Michael Allen's SAM model, and found that while it's been an improvement over ISD, SAM lacks the lightweight, adaptable approach to development.

In the next chapter, we'll learn about the core values that govern Agile along with its manifesto and guiding principles.

CHAPTER THREE
The Agile Manifesto

In this chapter we're going to discuss the Agile Manifesto. Once you complete this chapter, you'll be able to make training development decisions that are more closely aligned with the values of Agile. So, let's roll up our sleeves and start.

What exactly is the Agile Manifesto? Simply stated, it's a statement of core values and beliefs about how to best go about developing software. As we discussed earlier, the founders of Agile saw that the current approaches had numerous shortcomings.

In 2001, a group of these developers met at a ski resort in Utah to reflect and determine what values and principles would help them (and others) find better ways of developing software.[4] They decided to document these core values and principles and the result was the Agile Manifesto. It opens with the following message:

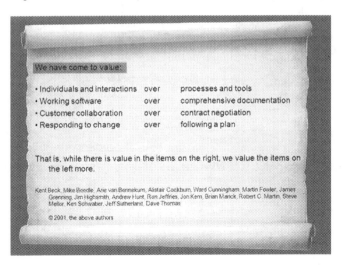

We have come to value:

* Individuals and interactions over processes and tools
* Working software over comprehensive documentation
* Customer collaboration over contract negotiation
* Responding to change over following a plan

That is, while there is value in the items on the right, we value the items on the left more.

Kent Beck, Mike Beedle, Arie van Bennekum, Alistair Cockburn, Ward Cunningham, Martin Fowler, James Grenning, Jim Highsmith, Andrew Hunt, Ron Jeffries, Jon Kern, Brian Marick, Robert C. Martin, Steve Mellor, Ken Schwaber, Jeff Sutherland, Dave Thomas

© 2001, the above authors

---

[4]   http://agilemanifesto.org/history.html

We are uncovering better ways of developing software by doing it and helping others do it. Through this work we have come to value: Individuals and interactions over processes and tools, Working software over comprehensive documentation, Customer collaboration over contract negotiation, Responding to change over following a plan. That is, while there is value in the items on the right, we value the items on the left more.[5]

Notice that the general spirit these developers hold dear is captured in the first statement of the manifesto: "We are uncovering better ways of developing software by doing it and helping others do it."

Essentially, the founders of Agile are acknowledging that the development process will never be perfect and that there will always be the need for continuous tweaks and improvements. They also suggest that ongoing collaboration among developers will take everyone much farther than going it alone. The Agile Manifesto offers four guiding values:[6]

- Individuals and interaction over processes and tools
- Working software over comprehensive documentation
- Customer collaboration over contract negotiation
- Responding to change over following a plan

Let's delve a bit deeper into each.

Individuals and interaction over processes and tools

"Individuals and interaction over processes and tools" doesn't mean that we should disregard process or tools. What it does

---

[5]   See http://agilemanifesto.org
[6]   Ibid.

suggest is this: if you have the ability or opportunity to choose, it's always better to interact with individuals than blindly follow a nonhuman process or tool. This means actually talking and listening to teammates and customers versus disregarding their input just to move on quicker to the next step. It means picking up the phone and having a conversation. With *Agile* you should start with the people and then decide what level of process and tools is necessary for a given circumstance. In other words, maximum the talents of your people and minimize your dependence on process and tools.

Working software over comprehensive documentation

This second value statement suggests that time is better served building a solution and getting customer feedback versus investing that same time and energy on building nothing but piles of documentation (only to find out deep into the process that the customer's needs have changed). Like all Agile key values, this proclamation isn't implying you skip documentation altogether, but to carefully build and ship in increments so the customer and delivery team are on a mutual path of confident progress.

Customer collaboration over contract negotiation

Valuing customer collaboration over contract negotiation is the third overarching value. Waterfall projects typically begin with investing a lot of time on the front-end determining rules of engagement, roles and responsibilities, risk management plans, etc. This value speaks for itself. Agile founders believe that during development projects, too much time is spent focusing on the contract, documenting the processes, scopes of work, change management process, and more. Contracts are necessary, yes. Too often, however, considerable energy is wasted trying to enforce those agreements instead of working together to figure out what needs to happen to get the product to market. A flexible approach to contracts gives both parties room to breathe when the inevitable changes arise.

With any project, stuff is going to happen. Changes are going to be required. People are going to drop the ball. The Agile founders understand that time is better spent collaborating with individuals in order to work through any issues versus forcing everyone to follow the original Statement of Work (SOW).

Responding to change over following a plan

We make plans but life happens. When was the last time you ran a project where nothing changed? Agile people understand: change happens and there's no way to avoid it.

I agree with them. It's better to do whatever it takes to respond to and accommodate change as opposed to sticking with a rigid plan that will likely deliver an ineffective solution.

With any project there's always a need for process and tools, documentation, contracts, and a plan. This fourth and final statement of the Agile Manifesto acknowledges that some planning is good; however, in the spirit of Agile's active, adaptable approach, the higher value is on the people, the working software, collaboration, and the capacity to easily respond to and address changes—while making good progress.

Chapter 3 Summary

We discussed the values and principles, known as the Agile Manifesto, which the founders put forth in order to deliver better software. We learned that the Agile process is always evolving, and that it values interaction over processes and tools, working software over comprehensive documentation, customer collaboration over contract negotiation, and responding to change over following a plan. Applying this philosophy to your training development efforts will make a huge positive impact on how your team operates and delivers. In the next chapter, we're going to discuss the principles that govern Agile. See you there.

CHAPTER FOUR
Agile Principles

The primary definition of "principle," according to *Merriam Webster*, is "a moral rule or belief that helps you know what is right and wrong and that influences your actions." Per the Agile Manifesto, there are twelve overarching principles that expand on the four key values and more fully explain what Agile is all about. In this chapter, we'll learn about these principles and how they can impact your training and development approach.

The twelve principles are as follows:[7]

1. Our highest priority is to satisfy the customer through early and continuous delivery of valuable software.

2. Welcome changing requirements, even late in development. Agile processes harness change for the customer's competitive advantage.

3. Deliver working software frequently, from a couple of weeks to a couple of months, with a preference to the shorter timescale.

4. Business people and developers must work together daily throughout the project.

5. Build projects around motivated individuals. Give them the environment and support they need, and trust them to get the job done.

---

[7] http://agilemanifesto.org/principles.html

6. Agile processes promote sustainable development. The sponsors, developers, and users should be able to maintain a constant pace indefinitely.

7. Working software is the primary measure of progress.

8. The most efficient and effective method of conveying information to and within a development team is face-to-face conversation.

9. Continuous attention to technical excellence and good design enhances agility.

10. Simplicity—the art of maximizing the amount of work not done—is essential.

11. The best architectures, requirements, and designs emerge from self-organizing teams.

12. At regular intervals, the team reflects on how to become more effective, then tunes and adjusts its behavior accordingly.

Here's what these principles mean to trainers:

Principle 1: Our highest priority is to satisfy the customer through early and continuous delivery of valuable software.

The first Agile principle states that "Our highest priority is to satisfy the customer through early and continuous delivery of valuable software." In other words above all else, the team should deliver software that customers deem valuable as quickly as possible and that the team should continue delivering valuable software.

Principle 2: Welcome changing requirements, even late in development. Agile processes harness change for the customer's competitive advantage.

Principle 2 says, unlike traditional approaches to software development where huge amounts of analysis and documentation need to be completed before a project starts, Agile limits this need by understanding that requirements will change and, as a result of this change, the customer will receive a better quality product. Agile therefore seeks to harness this change so that the customer gets the best product possible.

Principle 3: Deliver working software frequently, from a couple of weeks to a couple of months, with a preference to the shorter timescale.

The goal of Agile is to deliver frequent increments of working software so that customers can enjoy maximum usage of a product without waiting years for updates.

Principle 4: Business people and developers must work together daily throughout the project.

This principle highlights the need for frequent, ongoing collaboration between the business and product developers. Close interaction cuts down silos.

Principle 5: Build projects around motivated individuals. Give them the environment and support they need, and trust them to get the job done.

Build projects around motivated individuals. Give them the environment and support they need, and trust them to get the job done means that your most motivated employees should be the ones that staff your Agile teams. Management must foster a culture that allows them to make decisions and must also be willing to stand by the decisions that the team makes. Nothing can undermine an Agile team quicker than a manager that vetoes a team's recommendation.

Principle 6: The most efficient and effective method of conveying information to and within a development team is face-to-face conversation.

Whenever possible, meetings and interactions should take place in person. If the meetings cannot be held in person, video conferencing should be utilized.

Principle 7: Working software is the primary measure of progress.

Working software is the primary measure of progress not how many tasks have been completed. In Agile a team might have completed 99 out of the 100 tasks required to complete a project but the team is not seen as having made any progress at all unless they have delivered software that works.

Principle 8: Agile processes promote sustainable development. The sponsors, developers, and users should be able to maintain a constant pace indefinitely.

In other words Agile strives to create an environment where the pace of constant and frequent updates are maintained over a long period of time. This is in opposition to other process improvement programs where improvements are gained but not maintained.

Principle 9: Continuous attention to technical excellence and good design enhances agility.

There must be ongoing focus on the project's technical aspects. In Agile excellent design and technical quality go hand in hand. This principle highlights the commitment that Agile team members must have to continually evaluate the design of their solutions and their willingness to improve the technical functionality.

Principle 10: Simplicity—the art of maximizing the amount of work not done—is essential.

Keeping it simple is the key to getting things done and done quickly. Agile teams should make every attempt to develop the simplest solution possible.

Principle 11: The best architectures, requirements, and designs emerge from self-organizing teams.

The team needs to make all design and development decisions, not the manager alone. In Agile, teams determine how they are organized and how they interact. The role of the manager is simply to remove obstacles.

Principle 12: At regular intervals, the team reflects on how to become more effective, then tunes and adjusts its behavior accordingly.

The team should meet regularly, frequently. These meetings need activities built-in that allow the team to reflect on how they might improve. The team must then modify how it operates.

Chapter 4 Summary

We learned about the twelve Agile principles and how each might impact your approach to training and development. In the next chapter, we'll learn about two of the more popular approaches or flavors of Agile.

CHAPTER FIVE
Agile Methodologies

Some experts suggest that Agile development is more of a philosophy than a methodology. That said, there are a number of successful approaches to Agile development. These include extreme programming or XP, dynamic system development method or DSDM, Standard & Poor's, adaptive software development, and Scrum. While providing an overview of each of these approaches here, the remainder of this book focuses on the Scrum methodology.

Extreme Programming (XP)

In an extreme programming or XP project, programmers and business managers write what are called "user stories" on index cards. A user story is one or more sentences written in everyday language that describes what the user needs to be able to do. Each story describes a piece of the development and the amount of time it will take. This is similar to instructional designers writing learning objectives on index cards along with how the designer intends to address that objective and how long it will take to build the learning asset or intervention. With XP, the stories are set on a storyboard in order of priority. If the stories exceed the amount of time allotted for the project, then a Scrum master or project manager must decide what stories to delete. With XP, one story must be completely developed and finished before starting another. Team coding is best with the XP approach to Agile. In the training space this could mean that the entire learning team works to complete all of the learning solutions required in order to ensure the mastery of one learning objective before they began developing interventions for the rest of the learning objectives.

Dynamic System Development Method (DSDM)

Think of it as XP's progenitor. Popular in the United Kingdom, DSDM preaches two-to-six-week cycles, small development teams, and minimal requirements with the expectation these will change. But unlike other Agile techniques, DSDM also borrows more heavily from traditional development. A DSDM project even starts with a feasibility study that includes some of the planning and requirements tactics of traditional development.

Standard & Poor's (S&P)

Standard & Poor's has institutionalized its own Agile methodology. Their approach is similar to XP but with less focus on team coding and more on limiting project scope. In other words, S&P hasn't fully embraced celebrating change (even late in the process). They have an entire group that controls scope changes and no one practicing the S&P brand of Agile is allowed to change the scope unilaterally.

Adaptive Software Development

The Adaptive Software Development's version of Agile boxes the time to complete releasable software in two- to six-week cycles. Small development teams work with minimal requirements with the expectation that requirements will change. In a training space such as this, learning teams have two to six weeks to complete a piece of a larger learning solution—knowing that the user requirements are likely to change. Unlike other Agile techniques, adaptive software development borrows heavily from traditional development. Adaptive software development projects begin with a feasibility study that includes some of the planning and requirements tactics of traditional development.

Scrum

For this book, we'll be focusing on the Scrum methodology. Scrum uses time-boxed monthly increments called "sprints," with each sprint devoted to developing features collected in a list of requirements called a "backlog." In Scrum meetings (essentially a triage) the team gathers daily to ascertain the project's progress. To get a visual metaphor of Scrum, consider the following comparison:

A Tale of Two Sports

Close your eyes for a second and visualize a relay race. The runners get set in their starting blocks. The gun goes off. The contestants start running, batons in hand, racing to hand off that baton to their anxiously awaiting teammate. The baton is passed from runner to runner until the "anchor" or last runner on the team, crosses the finish line. A well-run relay race is a thing of beauty. When runners are in sync and handoffs go smoothly, there's no other track and field event quite as exciting. A problem arises, however, when the handoffs don't go smoothly, and the baton is dropped or, when one teammate has a bad day. When this happens, the entire team loses and there's nothing the other athletes can do to change the course. If the runner on the third leg (of the relay) wants to make an adjustment, there's no easy way to communicate this to the next runner starting the race. Now consider the dynamics of a rugby match. Not as artistic as the relay. Team members are bunched together into something called a scrum. The entire formation moves together. It moves slowly to the left, then right. Sometimes the formation moves forward, other times backward. Suddenly, the entire team sprints rapidly toward the goal, and then, they bunch into a scrum again. This is followed by another sprint and yet another scrum. Their close proximity allows players to communicate strategic changes to the team, at the same time. If one team member has a bad day, the others can still adapt, adjust, and compensate.

The Training Development Relay Race

Current approaches to instructional design resemble a relay race more than a rugby match. The process begins when a business partner contacts the training department about a possible training project. Someone from the training group then meets with the business partner to gather some initial requirements. The requirements are then passed to another team member who conducts a needs analysis and produces a design document. The design document gets passed off to someone responsible for creating a prototype. The prototype is then handed off to a team member for testing. The finish line is finally crossed when the business partner approves the training program. One big problem with this approach is that as the virtual baton gets passed from team member to team member, it's highly likely that the initial requirements will change and adjustments will need to be made. As Bob Mosher, chief learning evangelist at Ontuitive pointed out in the November 12, 2012 issue of *Chief Learning Officer* magazine, "Change is constant." We need to "examine how we design our content" and "who we involve." When changes occur, the serial nature of the current processes makes it difficult to communicate with the entire team in a way that allows everyone to make appropriate adjustments. The siloed nature of the work makes it challenging, if not impossible, for team members to compensate and assist other team members.

A Scrum Approach

Consider how the instructional design process would play out if it more closely resembled the rugby match that we illustrated earlier. The entire team would huddle with the customer to jointly identify the project's requirements. The team would then meet together in scrums in order to jointly come up with a strategy. Once the strategy was agreed to, the team would sprint forward to complete the agreed-upon tasks. Periodically, they would come together in scrums to access progress, identify changes, and make strategy adjustments. If the customer changed his or her requirements, the entire team would hear about it at the same time during one of the Scrum sessions. The team would, therefore, be in a better position to examine the implications of these changes, holistically. Designer and developer would be positioned to quickly devise an approach to address a change in learning requirements. They could jointly decide how to account for the addition of a new audience segment. If they were using the relay-race approach it's highly likely they wouldn't even know the requirements had changed until they'd presented their "completed" project. If the person responsible for testing the links in a new e-learning course called for some extra hands, in order for the testing to be completed by the scheduled date, the entire team would need to know. The team would, therefore, be positioned to assist this individual in testing so that the deliverable promise was met. Now contrast this to a waterfall approach in which team members simply receive an email informing them that testing will take an additional week. A rugby match might not be as pleasant to watch as a relay race, but if you're interested in reducing the communication gaffes of your instructional design process, you might just consider dropping the baton, picking up a rugby ball, and Scrumming it.

Chapter 5 Summary

In chapter five, we introduced you to a variety of approaches for implementing Agile. You learned about extreme programming or XP, dynamic system development method or DSDM, Standard & Poor's, adaptive software development, and the approach that we'll focus on for the rest of the book, Scrum.

Section One Summary

Congratulations, you've completed Section One of *Agile Methodology for Developing & Measuring Learning*. This section gave you the background specifics you need to finish the course. You learned that: The topic of Agile is important largely because today's consumers are more demanding. They expect instant access to information, frequent updates, and flawless performance, with every business and product they interact with. The Agile approach to development can help businesses meet these high, ever-changing expectations. You learned that it's important for training organizations to embrace Agile because training today is facing the same challenges that motivated software developers to adopt Agile years ago. You learned that the Agile approach to development is flexible and can rapidly respond to frequent change. It uses the least amount of documentation necessary to deliver a high-quality product. It minimizes up-front planning because planning is continuous and involves the whole team. You now know that Agile also allows changes to be made even late in the process and that the Agile approach provides tight feedback loops. You also learned about a previous attempt to apply iteration to the training and development process called the SAM model, championed by Dr. Michael Allen. You were also introduced to the philosophy of Agile development as stated in its manifesto of four key values and twelve principles. Finally, you were introduced to some of the more popular approaches to Agile implementation. In Section Two we'll walk you through the Agile process and talk about the roles associated with Agile, the tools or artifacts used, and the events or meetings that Agile team members attend.

SECTION TWO
The Scrum Process

By now you should be ready to walk through the Scrum process. In Section One we made the case for Agile. We talked about why the topic is important, gave some background on the process and its philosophy, and looked at the most popular approach used today to develop training, then established why it's not a good fit for today's business environment.

In this section we'll do a walk-through of the Agile development process. You'll learn about the roles of individuals that work on Agile teams. You'll be able to identify the artifacts used by Agile practitioners and the different types of meetings team members attend. Most importantly, you'll be able to identify step-by-step what must be accomplished when you use Agile.

It would take forever to take you through all of the different approaches to Agile, so for this book we'll focus solely on the Scrum methodology, the roles of the individuals in a Scrum implementation, the artifacts that are used, the events that take place, and how measurement is performed.

CHAPTER SIX

Scrum Roles, Artifacts, and Events

One of the beautiful things about Scrum is its simplicity. Scrum doesn't use a lot of moving parts. In fact, the entire process can be summed up in one short jingle or cheer . . .

"333 RAE"

With Scrum, the process of developing products and, at least for our purposes, creating learning solutions is accomplished using only three (3) roles, three (3) artifacts, and three (3) events or meetings. Otherwise known as 333 RAE. R is for roles, A for artifacts, and E for events. Let's start with the three roles that individuals involved with Scrum might play.

What roles exist in Scrum?

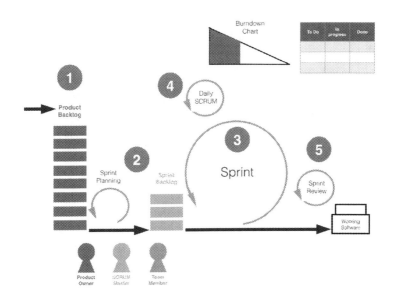

This image above shows the entire ecosystem of the Scrum process. As you can see, only three roles exist: product owner, Scrum master, and team member. Let's take a look at each discuss how they interact with the Scrum process.

Product Owner

The product owner is ideally a member of the organization or business unit, that's requesting the software, or asking for training. It's not uncommon, however, to have a proxy product owner. A proxy product owner is a member of the Scrum team who's responsible for representing the voice of the customer. The product owner, however, is responsible for ensuring that the right solution is defined, and the customer represented.

The product owner also clarifies business requirements and prioritizes deliverables. He or she typically spends about half their time with the customer and half with the Scrum team. In short, the product owner determines what needs to get done and what items have highest priority. They, however, never function as the "boss" of the Scrum team.

Scrum Master

The next role in a Scrum implementation is the Scrum master. While the product owner owns the "what," the Scrum master facilitates the "how." The Scrum master oversees the process used to build the solution or create the training. He or she serves the team by removing impediments, coaching the team on Scrum practices, and facilitating the events that take place during the course of a Scrum project. Like the product owner, the Scrum master is not the "boss" of the development team.

Team Member

The final role in Scrum is that of team member. Scrum teams should consist of no more than seven members who are by nature, cross-functional. In a training implementation of Scrum this means that programmers, technical writers, graphic artists, instructional designers, and instructional technicians all work together to deliver for the customer. As stated previously, with Agile, team members organize themselves and are free to make whatever adjustments are required to deliver.

What artifacts exist in Scrum?

Now let's talk about the three artifacts or tools used to manage the entire Scrum process. These include the product backlog, the sprint backlog, and the burn-down chart. Here's how each relate to the Scrum ecosystem.

Product Backlog

Product backlog is a prioritized list of customer requirements or learning outcomes that must ultimately be converted into learning solutions. Think of this as a "what's on my plate?" Now remember, as we said earlier, the determining of "what's" on the product backlog and "how" those requirements are prioritized is the product owner's responsibility; however, this is typically facilitated by the Scrum master with team members possibly assisting.

Sprint Backlog

Sprint backlog is the list of learning solutions the team is committed to completing during a given "sprint" or iteration. If the product backlog is what's on your plate, think of the sprint backlog as what you're going to eat first. Ensuring that the sprint backlog accurately reflects what the team can accomplish during the sprint or time-boxed development period is the responsibility of the Scrum master.

Burn-Down Chart

The final artifact used to manage a Scrum project is the burn-down chart. This tool is used to track the progress of the work completed during a sprint.

What events exist in Scrum?

Scrum team members only attend three types of meetings: sprint planning, daily standup or daily Scrum, and sprint review. Here's a description of each of these important events.

Sprint Planning

The goal of sprint planning is to get agreement on what the team is committed to developing and putting into production (or make available for customers) at the completion of the next sprint or time-boxed development period. In other words, decide what items move from the product backlog to the sprint backlog. We'll discuss how to conduct a sprint planning session in a later chapter.

Daily Scrum

Daily Scrum is a 10–15 minute meeting that takes place every day of sprint. It's used to document the progress of work and identify any impediments to tasks being completed. These meetings should typically take place at the same time, in the same location, daily.

Sprint Review

Sprint review is typically divided into two parts. The first half is used to demonstrate to the customer what's been accomplished and have them accept the deliverables; the second half is strictly for team members only so everyone can reflect on how the sprint went and recommit to making any necessary adjustments to help the next iteration run smoother.

Chapter 6 Summary

We learned about the roles, artifacts, and events that facilitate the Scrum process. We uncovered that the entire Scrum ecosystem consists of three roles (product owner, Scrum master, and team member); three artifacts (product backlog, sprint backlog, and burn-down chart); and three events (sprint planning, daily Scrum, and sprint review). In the next chapter, we'll explain how each of those roles, artifacts, and events interact with the Scrum process.

CHAPTER SEVEN
The Scrum Process

In the last chapter we talked about the roles, artifacts, and events associated with Scrum. Next we'll examine how each of these interacts with steps in the process. An easy way to remember the steps is to use the jingle: backlog, plan, sprint, scrum, review and repeat.

Backlog

The first step in the Agile Scrum process is the creation or grooming of the product backlog. As we pointed out earlier, a product backlog is a prioritized list of all requirements that must ultimately be turned into learning solutions. Creating and maintaining this list is the responsibility of the product owner. The Scrum master, however, facilitates this step in the process, and it's not uncommon for members of the development team to also participate.

The goal of backlog planning is to identify all the known product requirements (or learning outcomes), estimate how long they'll take to develop, and then prioritize those requirements or learning outcomes in order of importance. Later on, we'll teach you how to conduct a backlog—planning meeting; but for now, just know that you'll frequently find the initial requirements vague and too large to easily estimate. When that happens, the requirements or learning outcomes will need to be distilled into smaller requirements for estimations.

Plan

Once the product backlog has been established, the next step is to plan and commit to the backlog items from which the team can turn into learning solutions during the next two—to four-week time-boxed cycle (called a sprint or iteration). This step is called sprint planning and includes the entire development team.

During sprint planning, the items in the product backlog (those with highest priority that can also be completed within the time-boxed period of the iteration) are moved from product backlog to sprint backlog. If an item is too large to be completed in the time-boxed constraints of the sprint, it must be reduced into smaller items or deliverables that can be completed given the constraints.

Sprint

Once the sprint backlog is established, the next step is to begin working toward developing and delivering agreed-upon solutions. This is called the sprint. As we noted earlier, a sprint is a time-boxed work cycle that runs typically from two to four weeks. Here's where team members code, develop, write, and engage in order to produce the end product agreed to during sprint planning.

Scrum

Each day of sprint, the development team convenes for no more than 10–15 minutes in order to accomplish what's called the daily standup or daily Scrum. During this meeting each team member answers three questions:

What did you complete yesterday?

What are you going to complete today?

Is there any impediment that might prevent you from accomplishing what you're committed to?

During this meeting, the Scrum master ensures that progress is updated accordingly on the burn-down chart.

Review

Once the sprint is complete, the team attends another meeting called the sprint review or retrospective. Its purpose is to demonstrate to the customer all the solutions completed during the sprint and to discuss ways to improve the next sprint.

Some organizations split this review session into two separate meetings: one customer meeting to demonstrate deliverables and gain acceptance (usually called the sprint retrospective); and the second meeting attended by team members only. This allows team members to freely discuss what worked (and didn't) with the recently completed sprint and to identify what adjustments to make to improve the next sprint.

Repeat

In any event, once the sprint review is complete, the entire process repeats itself.

Chapter 7 Summary

We walked you through the Scrum process. You now know what roles exist in the Scrum version of Agile, what artifacts or tools are used to manage the effort, and what types of events or meetings exist in Scrum. You also now know how those roles, artifacts, and events work together to complete the required steps in Scrum.

In the next chapter we'll show you how to develop a product backlog. See you there.

CHAPTER EIGHT
Establishing a Product Backlog

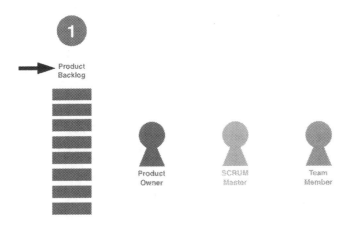

As we discussed in previous chapters, developing a product backlog is the first step in the Agile Scrum process. Product backlog is a prioritized list of all requirements that must ultimately become learning solutions. Creating and maintaining this list is the product owner's responsibility. The Scrum master, however, facilitates this step in the process, and often members of the development team also participate.

Steps to establishing a product backlog

The goal of backlog planning is to identify all the known product requirements (or learning outcomes), estimate how long they'll take to develop, and then prioritize those requirements or learning outcomes in order of importance. There are essentially six steps involved with creating and grooming a product backlog:

1. List all known projects

2. Add any new projects

3. Remove any canceled projects

4. Prioritize the projects

5. Gain a deeper understanding of the projects in terms of complexity, size, and delivery

6. Break it down into smaller components

Let's look at how these steps might work in practice . . .

Step 1: List all known projects

The team would first sit down and list all known work or projects on paper, word software, or spreadsheet. This list should include all training projects that are in progress as well as any business initiatives that might require a learning intervention. Also, add the appropriate business initiative to any "in progress" training project. Including this information now comes in handy later when you need to demonstrate the impact your learning solutions have had on the organization.

Backlog Worksheet

Business Initiative	Priority (1-10)	Possible Learning Solutions	T-Shirt Size	Estimate of Effort Required (Hrs)
Employee Engagement				
Product Update				

The image above is a sample Training Scrum product backlog worksheet. We'll explain how each column is used as we move through this section. At this point, however, it's important to understand that the "Business Initiative" column must be completed from the perspective of the business, not T+D's. As an example, you'd only list employee engagement under "Business Initiative" if there were a corporate initiative to improve employee engagement that might possibly require a learning intervention.

Step 2: Add any new projects

Once all the known projects are listed, the next step is to add any new projects. If this were a backlog grooming session, the team would start here.

Step 3: Remove any canceled projects

At this point, any canceled projects should also be removed from the list. We'll talk about how to address delayed projects a little later, but let's assume the product owner tells us that the Regulatory Relations project has been canceled and, therefore, will not require learning support. That project would then be removed or crossed off the list.

Step 4: Prioritize the projects

Once there's clarity around workload size and/or how many projects are waiting in the backlog, the project owner then works with the team to prioritize projects. Again, if this were a grooming session, the product owner would make the team aware of any changes in priority.

Prioritizing should be based on relativity. As an example, the Scrum master might ask, "How important is the regulatory relations effort to the business, in relationship to the new product rollout?" "Or, if we could only support one effort, which one would we support? The new product rollout or product update?" These types of queries would continue until the product owner and team were both comfortable with how the projects are being prioritized.

Step 5: Gain a deeper understanding of the projects

The next step is to gain a deeper understanding of the projects. This requires the team to get clarity on a few things, such as how complicated this project might be, how big, and what is the deadline. Since the product owner sets the due dates, we'll focus the rest of this section on techniques for estimating how complicated and big initiatives might become. Remember, we always start with the highest priority project as identified by the product owner. In this example, it's a new product rollout.

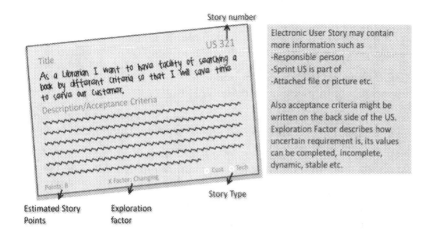

User Stories

One way to gain a deeper understanding of the project is to write what Agile calls "user stories" for each business initiative. Instructional designers should be very familiar with this approach because it's simply another way of stating that we need to understand the ABCDs of the initiative: Audience, Behavior, Condition, Degree. For each initiative, the team identifies the learning intervention audience, what behaviors need to be demonstrated, what conditions support those behaviors, and to what degree they need to accomplish them. There are entire books and courses on how to write good learning objectives. For this course, we won't go into great detail, but here's how it might work . . .

Questioning or interviewing the product owner accomplishes the goal of identifying the audience for the business initiative. For this example, let's assume the product owner has just explained that the new product being rolled out is a mobile banking app, and that there are two customer bases: 1) retail customers who'll use the app, and 2) help or service desk agents to support the app.

The interview continues and the team uncovers two behaviors that retail customers exhibit: 1) logging onto the system, and 2) setting up their profiles. That means the help agents must be able to: 1) reset passwords, and 2) unlock accounts. This information is then added to the worksheet.

Be prepared for some back and forth discussion with this activity, and with every worksheet component. Experience has shown that this effort is rarely a "one-and-done." Typically, it calls for frequent iterations.

The team then continues to question the product owner to uncover what conditions exist whenever these particular behaviors are exhibited. In this example, conditions for the retail customer are as follows: given an iPhone with an app installed and Internet connectivity, one condition for the help agent might be to have access to the customer's admin panel and all required verification information.

Learning Solution Worksheet

Business Initiative	Audience	Behaviors	Condition	Degree	Potential Solution
New Product Rollout					

The next task: uncover to what degree the audience members need to perform these tasks. In the case of logging onto the system, the product owner explains that retail customers must be able to complete login in no more than three attempts or else they'll be locked out.

This Q&A (or interviewing) continues until the team has identified as many of the audience members, behaviors, conditions, and degrees for as many of the business initiatives as they can, working from items of highest priority to lowest.

Once the audience, behaviors, conditions, and degrees are determined, the team can then take an initial pass at identifying potential learning solutions for each outcome.

Business Initiative	Audience	Behaviors	Condition	Degree	Potential Solution
New Product Rollout	Retail Customers	Log onto system	Given an iphone with mobile app installed	Given an iphone with mobile app installed	•simulation •userguide •help file
		Create a profile	After being logged into the system	With all required fields compete	•simulation •userguide •help file
	Help center agents	Reset customer passwords	•Given access to customer admin panel •Given customer verification information	within 1 minute	•quick tip •FAQ
		Unlock customer accounts	•Given access to customer admin panel •Given customer verification information	within 3 minutes	•product simulation •quick tip

This is where team members with instructional design (ID) backgrounds can take the lead. For example, the designer suggests that a product simulation, user guide, and help file might be the best approach to teaching this particular learning outcome. At this point in the process, there's less team debate because it's likely that the ultimate solutions might change. The goal here is to get a sense of how much work is required to build the solution. The process of identifying potential learning solutions continues until these solutions are identified according to the highest priority items.

How Big Is This?

Now that we have a sense of how complicated the project is and what types of learning solutions might be appropriate, we can take a first pass at estimating the effort required to build these solutions and ultimately determine how much "effort" exists in the product backlog. One method of rough estimating is to try the concept of "T-shirt sizing."

Just like prioritizing, T-shirt sizing relies on a relative measure. The team looks at the potential learning solutions for each business initiative, assigning a T-shirt size to each. We recommend using just three sizes: small, large, and 3xl.

The team examines every learning solution they might build in order to support the business initiative the customer has identified as the highest priority item; they then make a determination of the "size" (or how much effort is required to build the solution) based on the T-shirt criteria. In this example, there are a lot of learning solutions that must be developed in order to support the new product rollout and the project is fairly complex. So we're assigning this effort a 3xl.

Business Initiative	Priority (1-10)	Possible Learning Solutions	T-Shirt Size	Estimate of Effort Required (Hrs)
Employee Engagement	7	•Webinars •Video tips		
Product Update	9	•update existing help files •update existing e-learning		
New Product Rollout	**10**	• 2 product simulations •quick tips •userguide •help file •FAQs	3X	
Leadership Development	8	•e-Learning courses •Mentoring		
Regulatory Relations	5			

In comparison, the work that's required to handle updates to support the product update initiative is simple, straightforward, and small; therefore, the team assigns a small T-shirt. Once all the initiatives are rated, the team then assigns an estimated effort to each size. Many organizations assign an hourly estimate of work effort to a T-shirt size before they even begin sizing; for example, the organization might determine in advance that a large T-shirt equates to 200 hours of effort, and a 3xl, 600 hours.

T-Shirt Size Poker

A fun approach to sizing is to play T-Shirt Size Poker. With this approach, the Scrum master deals three cards, each with a different size, to each team member. The Scrum master then identifies an initiative and asks each team member to show the card they think corresponds to the size of the effort. Let's say, for example, that three team members identify the effort as small and two see it as a 3xl, so the team discusses the rationale behind each choice. Once they reach a consensus the team moves to the next item. This continues until everyone agrees on a size estimate for all items.

How much can we do?

The next team step, called a sprint or iteration, is to determine what learning solutions for the new product rollout can be built and delivered to customers within a two-week period. Note: Two weeks is certainly not a rule of thumb; each organization must determine for itself how log their sprints will be.

	Team Member	Team Member	Team Member	Team Member
Gross Hrs.	80	80	80	80
Non-Project Meetings	6	10	4	2
Project Meetings	8	8	8	8
Vacation	16	0	8	40
Capacity	50	62	60	30

Total Capacity	202 hrs

We take the total available hours for the entire team and subtract the time that's unavailable for development work (including vacation time and meetings). In the following example, four team members have a total capacity of 202 hours available to work on the new product rollout during the next two weeks. But let's say the effort to support the new product rollout requires 600 hours.

There's no way every learning solution can be completed and delivered in that time frame. The team must therefore get clarity around what it will take to build each suggested learning solution, and then break them down into smaller deliverables.

Step 6: break it down into smaller components

In order to make the project more manageable we must first understand the priority of each learning solution and the effort required to develop it. Following the same approach that was used to gain a deeper understanding of the business initiative, the product owner prioritizes the deliverables and the team "sizes" the effort behind each.

Possible Learning Solution	Priority (1-10)	Description	T-Shirt Size	Estimate of Effort Required (Hrs)
Product Simulation 1	1	Logging into system General Navigation	SM	75
Product Simulation 2	3	Editing and	SM	75
Quick Tips	5	How to guide	SM	100
Userguide	7	How to manual for system users	LG	125
Help File	9	Help system for new product rollout	LG	175
FAQs	10	Handout to answer frequent questions	SM	75

As you can see from the image above, the product owner has identified the highest-priority learning solution as the FAQs. The team estimates that the effort to create these FAQs is 75 hours. Since we have 202 hours of capacity in this sprint, we can move the FAQs into the sprint backlog. The Help Files come next as the highest-priority deliverable, according to the product owner.

These will require 175 hours of work, putting the team over its workload capacity. One of two approaches can be taken to address this dilemma: 1) The product manager can re-prioritize and agree that the User Guides fall in line as the next highest priority for this sprint; or 2) the team can break the Help File system into smaller deliverables.

If the product owner decides that the Help Files must be included in this sprint, then the team dismantles the Help Files into smaller, more manageable components. In this example, the team divides the Help Files by topics, which are then prioritized by the product owner. The team assigns an estimated effort to these smaller deliverables, and then moves them into the sprint based on priority.

Chapter 8 Summary

We covered the steps required to establish a product backlog. You were introduced to tools and processes to assist you in gaining a greater understanding of the items in backlog and approaches to sizing. We talked about breaking down the project into smaller, more manageable components as well as techniques for understanding the capacity of your training team.

In the following chapter, we'll take a look at the activities that happen during sprint. Next!

CHAPTER NINE
The Sprint

As discussed in the previous chapter, the sprint (according to the Scrum process) is where the development work (or effort) to build the learning solutions that the team agrees to complete is done. In Agile, teams are self-directed so the approach used to build content varies from team to team. Events that occur during sprint are the daily standup and sprint review, and the artifact used is the burn-down chart. This chapter teaches you how to facilitate the daily standup and sprint review, as well as how to use the burn-down chart.

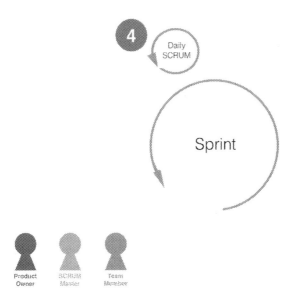

As stated earlier, a sprint is a time-boxed duration that is typically two to four weeks long. This is when team members code, develop, write, and engage in order to produce the learning solution agreed to during sprint planning.

The Daily Scrum

Each day of sprint, the development team meets for no more than 10–15 minutes in order to accomplish the Scrum event known as the daily standup or daily Scrum. The purpose of this meeting is two-fold: 1) assess the team's progress against commitments they've made; and 2) identify and remove any impediments that might prevent the team from making its deliverables. During this meeting each team member answers three questions:

1. What did you complete yesterday?

2. What are you going to complete today?

3. Is there any impediment that might prevent you from accomplishing what you're committed to?

By focusing on what each person accomplished yesterday as well as what will get done today, the entire team understands what's complete and what still needs attention.

Note: It's important to understand that the daily Scrum is not a status or update meeting where the boss collects information about who's behind schedule. It's also not a problem-solving meeting where the team discusses how to address issues. Allowing status updates and problem solving to creep into a daily standup will negatively affect the team's ability to be effective. In this meeting, team members are simply making commitments to each other. Not a boss.

If, for example, during a daily Scrum the graphic designer says, "Today, I will finish the graphics for module one," then everyone on the team knows that in tomorrow's meeting, he will say whether or not he finished the task. This helps the entire team realize the significance of these commitments as they're made to each other.

The Scrum master is responsible for resolving any raised impediments as quickly as possible. Some typical training impediments include:

- I don't have access to the system yet

- I still don't have the software I need

- The SME canceled the meeting

During the daily Scrum, the Scrum master ensures that ongoing progress is noted in the burn-down chart.

The Burn-Down Chart

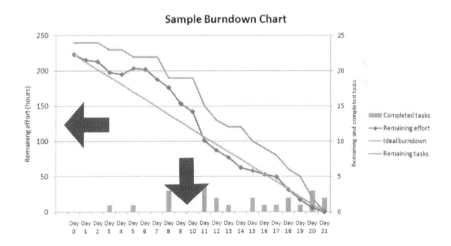

A burn-down chart is a graphical representation of the remaining work to complete. The outstanding work (or backlog) is often on a vertical axis, with time running horizontal. In this example above, the team is doing a three-week or twenty-one-day sprint. The Scrum master helps to facilitate the burn-down chart by moving work items not yet started from the to-do column into the in-progress column and moving completed items from the in-progress column to the done column. This effort gives the entire team a clear view of the progress and commitments being made.

The Sprint Review

Once the sprint is complete, the team attends another meeting called the sprint review or retrospective—the last event in the Scrum process The purpose of this meeting is to demonstrate the solutions completed during sprint to the customer and discuss how to improve the next sprint. Some organizations split the review session into two separate meetings: one customer meeting to demonstrate deliverables and gain acceptance (usually referred to as a sprint retrospective); and the second meeting attended by team members only. This allows team members to freely discuss what worked (and didn't work) with the recently completed sprint and to identify what adjustments are needed in order to improve the next sprint. Let's take a look at how these meetings might unfold . . .

Since the purpose of the sprint review is to demonstrate that the training solution was completed as well as to gain customer acceptance, all stakeholders must attend. In our example, the team made a commitment to deliver the entire FAQ document and Help Files (including specific topics). The team met next with the product owner and demonstrated how those products work, both in the context of overall strategy, as well as measured against any acceptance criteria previously agreed to.

There are essentially three possible outcomes of this meeting. The first is that the product owner accepts the learning solutions and asks the training team to deploy them into production. If this happens the training team makes the solution(s) available to customers and moves next to the sprint retrospective followed by the next sprint planning session.

The second possible outcome is that the product owner agrees that the solutions meet all of the acceptance criteria, but they want revisions. If this happens the solutions are considered complete but the requested updates are then placed into the product backlog and prioritized against other backlog items for work scheduling. This prioritization takes place at the next backlog grooming session.

The third and worst possible outcome is that the learning solutions do not meet the acceptance criteria and are rejected by the product owner. (This undesirable outcome likely leads to a very spirited sprint retrospective.) In any event, once the sprint review is complete, the training or development team convenes for a final meeting in order to discuss how they can improve the team's performance on the next sprint.

The Sprint Retrospective

The sprint retrospective meeting should follow the best practices of any "lessons learned" meeting including:

- Establishing shared ground rules

- Ensuring everyone has the opportunity to speak

- Giving individuals the opportunity to pass on speaking

- Highlighting what went well first

- Capturing all opportunities for improvement

- Voting on which items are critical for the next sprint

- Documenting and distributing the results

Once review and retrospective meetings are complete, the team repeats the Scrum process starting with backlog grooming.

Chapter 9 Summary

In this chapter we talked about the events and artifacts used during sprint. You learned that the daily standup or daily Scrum is used to help team members be accountable to each other and that the sprint review has a two-fold purpose: 1) demonstrate the learning solution(s) to the customer; and 2) identify ways of being more efficient. You also learned that the sprint retrospective is the last activity in the Scrum process before the process repeats itself.

SECTION THREE

A Case Study on Scrum in a Training Environment

DEVELOPING & MEASURING TRAINING THE AGILE WAY

(A Case Study)

In 2012, in an effort to realize an increase in customer satisfaction, highly engaged employees, greater visibility into the process of releases, improved ability to address change, and higher quality products, DTCC Learning changed their organizational structure and adopted Agile as the preferred approach for developing learning solutions. Here's a case study of that experience.

The Announcement

Change in management is one of the most difficult components of any leader's job, especially when it includes adjustments the leaders themselves must make themselves. The management team of DTCC Learning was unanimous: in order to better meet the needs of the business lines our customer training organization supported, the team needed to adapt an organizational structure and development methodology that better enabled rapid and iterative development, quick reaction to change, and closer customer collaboration.

The decision was made to restructure the organization. Instead of having designers report inside one silo, instructors in another, and business analysts in yet a third, teams of designers, instructors, analysts, and technologists would report into shared learning domains that were responsible for all learning support of specific lines of business.

The leadership team was also in agreement that the current "waterfall" approach to learning product development didn't allow us to react as quickly as needed to a rapidly changing business environment. With this new agreement in place, the date of the reorganization and timing of the Agile training was decided.

In conversations with my direct reports, there was excitement about the opportunity to evolve from roles where they'd been essentially expert technologists or instructional designers overseeing teams of technologists or designers—into roles that allowed them to become leaders of business units in which they were responsible for providing all learning solutions to a portfolio of product lines.

There was, however, some inevitable anxiety about their ability to perform well in these new roles. To make work life even trickier, staff members sensed something was "about to happen" and began to ask nervous questions. The rumors hit an all-time high when a meeting request was issued for a mandatory "all hands" meeting.

As our employees entered the meeting room, it was obvious everyone was on edge. I wasted no time getting to the point, explaining to everyone that I had called us together to announce reorganization. I briefly explained the rationale for the impending changes, which included team member feedback. With that, my assistant handed out a three-page document.

On page one (without staff names) was a graphic of the organization structure we'd operated in for the past several years. I quickly spoke about the positives and negatives of that structure. On page two (also minus any names) was a graphic representing this new structure. I then spent a few minutes speaking to the benefits of that configuration. Finally, page three presented the new structure with employee names assigned to teams.

Questions started flowing. Most had to do with workflow and process issues. I explained to the team that our new approach would be one where each team decided for themselves how to get the work done as opposed to an outdated methodology largely engineered by management and "pushed down" to them.

For employees who'd felt the burden of being constrained by the old process, I could see a visible sigh of relief. For those who took comfort in the familiar structure those processes provided, I observed nervous looks. The Q&A continued for the better part of forty-five minutes. At that point, I assured them that this change was a "win-win" for everyone and that I had confidence they'd make it work. I also provided the staff with all of my contact information and invited them to contact me in any way they felt comfortable with their questions, concerns, or simply wanting to talk.

I returned to my office expecting a long line of employees with gripes and plenty of voicemail messages expressing dissatisfaction. I waited about an hour and no one stopped by. Curious, I called one of my direct reports and he said the feedback had been very positive and, in fact, the staff was excited about these new possibilities. I did my customary follow-up calls and drive-by conversations to gather more feedback and got the same kind of messages.

I checked my e-mail and found several notes from staff thanking me for how the reorganization was handled and expressing excitement about the opportunities it offered. With Agile training scheduled for the following week, part one of our transition to developing and measuring our training approaches "the Agile way" had started on the right foot.

The Training, Part 1

Having made the case for the switch to Agile (communicating when it would happen and how it might affect both the organization and individuals), the next step was to ensure that all our team members had the necessary tools to implement this new approach. We accomplished this by training everyone in the Agile methodology.

We commissioned a vendor to serve as a coach. The leadership team then spent weeks describing to him the culture of our company, the nature of our customers, and the temperament of our staff.—The last thing the leadership team wanted was an "off-the-shelf" class on Agile. We felt that if Agile was going to be successful at DTCC, then the training had to be tailored to our specific needs.

Since this was (as far as we knew) the first time Agile would be applied to the development of learning solutions, DTCC Learning leadership wanted the training to contain examples specific to what we did, not some vague academic exercise. The vendors assured us they understood the nature of our work, and that by the end of the three-day session, the team would be well-prepared to start using Agile on current projects. The leadership team was especially confident because one of our colleagues had already implemented Agile at two other companies and had previously worked with the vendor.

Special care was taken to ensure that team members across all geographic locations had a good, interactive experience. Rooms with multiple HD cameras and high-powered microphones were secured. We had a test walk-through on the Friday prior to training and we seemed to be set for a successful session . . . when everything went wrong.

We found out that the rooms we'd tested and thought we'd reserved were actually scheduled for a town hall meeting. This left the team scrambling to secure alternate rooms and equipment. Even worse, just two days before the training event launched, the vendor informed us that the coach who'd spent so much time understanding our organization, culture, and workflow had a family emergency and wouldn't be able to deliver the training. We had to hire a backup trainer, and suddenly, the real-world exercises and examples we'd been expecting from the original trainer were now a thing of the past.

These misfortunes resulted in the team spending three days in suboptimal facilities receiving an academic off-the-shelf lecture on Agile. As Dwight D. Eisenhower once said: "Plans are useless, planning however is invaluable." Careful preparations for the training session allowed us to avert what might have been a catastrophe. In the next section, I'll cover what happened that allowed us to dodge failure along with what we learned from the training session.

The Training, Part 2

The Eisenhower quote was totally applicable to what the DTCC Learning team had experienced with Agile training. After months of carefully planning every aspect of the learning experience, in the end, the plans became useless as a result of factors beyond our control: the reserved facilities were no longer available and the preferred instructor was out. This exercise in planning, however, ultimately allowed the session to achieve most of our goals.

This experience empowered our leadership team to boldly stop the instructor and request that he provide more concrete examples. When the attendees at remote locations had a hard time seeing or hearing interactions at the primary site, the participants frequently requested that camera angles be changed or that comments be repeated. While the overall quality of the training left much to be desired, the team walked away with a basic understanding of some important tenants of Agile, an appreciation of how it could be used in a learning development environment, and a desire to start.

What Is Agile?

The frequent requests for examples allowed the DTCC Learning team to quickly learn that Agile was an iterative approach to development in which both the solutions and requirements evolve over time as a result of collaboration between cross-functional, self-organizing teams. This is quite different from the ADDIE model or even the Six Sigma approach. Both Six Sigma and ADDIE are waterfall methodologies, heavy in process and documentation. In waterfall approaches, the sequential plan determines cost and schedule. Agile, on the other hand, allows the vision and values to determine the schedule. Its framework is based on just three roles, four artifacts, and five events.

The 3 Roles

1. **Product Owner**—Responsible for what's developed, represents the customer's needs, defines the right solution, and prioritizes the work.

2. **Scrum Master**—Responsible for how work gets done, coaches the team, facilitates meetings, and removes obstacles.

3. **Development Team**—Cross-functional group responsible for completing the work.

The 3 Artifacts

1. **Product Backlog**—List of all features that must be delivered.

2. **Sprint Backlog**—List of all features being worked on for a particular release.

3. **Burn-Down Chart**—A tool used to view the progress of work being accomplished.

The 3 Events

1. **Sprint Planning Meeting**—Meeting to get agreement on what working software will be delivered during iteration.

2. **Daily Standup**—Short status meeting (10–15 minutes).

3. **Sprint Review/Retrospective**—Demonstration to customer of the items completed during sprint. Internal meeting held at the end of sprint to determine what went well and find ways of improving for the next sprint.

How Would Agile Work in Learning Organizations?

Ensuing discussions and questions uncovered that what the Agile approach does for learning organizations is this: instead of spending weeks or months analyzing (analysis) the problem to determine the learning solution, and then presenting those findings to a business partner for their approval, followed by the creation of a design document or outline and objectives (design) that are submitted for yet another review and approval, followed by the creation of a prototype (development) that needs to go through the same review and approval process (whew! are you still with me?), the team gets agreement on a set of features (learning outcomes) to accomplish, and as a result of the training, divides those features into prioritized work items—allowing the team to develop and deliver a working learning solution within two to four weeks!

All this caught the attention of the attendees visibly tired of processes that were heavy with reviews and approvals, and which frequently resulted in months of work becoming a waste of time as a result of changing requirements. With the Agile Manifesto, our staff bought into Agile even more so when they realized: individuals and personal interactions were valued over processes and tools, working software over comprehensive documentation, customer collaboration over contract negotiation, and nimble response to change over following an elaborate plan.

Now the Hard Part

The team left the training session both excited about using the Agile methodology and concerned that they didn't have enough concrete examples to get it right. The leadership team assured them that they didn't expect them to "get it right" immediately, only that they continue to perfect the approach. In the following pages, I'll be sharing the good, the bad, and the ugly of the DTCC Learning road to Agile.

Creating A Product backlog

The first task of the Agile methodology is to derive a list of product features that must be delivered to customers. In Agile, this list is called a product backlog, and once the DTCC Learning staff completed the Agile training, each of our three DTCC Learning domains set out to accomplish this task.

Creating a product backlog is typically handled by first meeting with the product owner or customer(s), having them articulate their vision for the product, translating that vision into features, and then prioritizing those. This, of course, is how it's articulated in the world of software development.

So while. the approach sounds simple and straightforward, accomplishing this in a training and development space proved more difficult. Each of the three DTCC Learning domains discovered that they faced a common set of challenges when attempting to create their first product backlog, including:

- How do we translate a language and approach meant for software development into something that makes sense for learning solution development?

- What do we do with work already in progress?

- How do we handle work not specific to any one line of business?

- How do we engage all the numerous product owners that we need to support?

- What do we do if a specific skill-set is missing from one of the development teams?

Old habits proved hard to break, and team members (at least initially) continued to look to their managers for answers. To the credit of our leadership team, my direct reports continued to challenge each of their teams to come up with plausible solutions to these challenges. My role was to ensure the organization that I did not expect things would be overnight perfect, and that it was absolutely OK (and natural) to make mistakes.

I walked the floor more frequently and encouraged individuals at every opportunity. I began sending weekly video podcasts that highlighted the good things happening across the organization. My direct reports constantly reminded us all that the Agile approach adopted here at DTCC must be unique and specific to the challenges we faced. Ultimately, each team was able to arrive at solutions to these common challenges, including:

How do we translate language and approaches meant for software development into something that makes sense for learning solution development?

As the teams became more familiar with Agile, translation became a non-issue. They simply started to substitute language that made sense in a learning development environment instead of software development.

What do we do with work already in progress?

The three learning domains were well positioned to address work already in progress. Since teams were largely comprised of individuals that previously supported the lines of business the domain was aligned with, much of the "in-progress work" immediately moved under the responsibility of the corresponding domain. Team members agreed that when there were exceptions, the individuals who'd started the work would see those projects through to completion.

How do we handle work that isn't specific to any one line of business?

Team members agreed that as cross-functional requests were entered into the organizational backlog, the team with the greatest capacity at that time would be responsible.

How do we engage all the numerous product owners we need to support?

There was no universal approach for this challenge. Instead, each learning domain adopted what worked best for that domain and the lines of businesses supported. One learning domain set up a series of consecutive meetings one day a week. Another arranged meetings with representatives from groups of businesses.

What do we do if a specific skill-set is missing from one of the development teams?

Team members from each domain agreed to provide cross-training whenever there was a skill deficit, as well as lend expertise to other domains as needed.

Within two weeks, each learning domain had met with their customers, established a prioritized product backlog, established operating procedures, and was prepared to begin their first "sprint." What made this effort different and so rewarding was that all of these activities were driven and accomplished by the team, not the manager. If nothing else positive happened as a result of our adaptation of Agile, the fact that teams and individuals were feeling more empowered was enough of a payoff.

The First Sprint

The newly formed DTCC Learning training teams began their first sprint with significant anguish. Although they'd been through Agile training and participated in creating a product backlog, none of the employees had ever developed learning products in this fashion. They felt uncomfortable attempting to recommend solutions without having "all the information."

Most were reluctant to committing to the timeframes required to complete the tasks identified. Many had problems distilling or breaking down learning solution recommendations into smaller learning assets that could be put into production immediately after the sprint was completed. Some felt that their team lacked the skill-set required to deliver on the necessary learning assets.

Anguish not withstanding, all teams performed admirably on their first sprint. One team released more learning solutions to customers after the first two-week sprint than the previous entire quarter. Another team committed to delivering 43 learning solutions and succeeded in publishing 36 of those items to production. What made the Agile sprint even more successful was that team members could self-identify obstacles that were preventing them from delivering 100 percent of the value they'd committed to, as well as develop plans for doing even better in the next sprint. The basic feedback was an overall sense of empowerment. Each learning team was energized and anticipated their next sprints.

The challenge for the leadership team now became maintaining this energy and analyzing the productivity and quality of the learning solutions that were produced pre—and post-Agile.

Early Results

The early results of the Agile implementation exceeded our expectations. The average number of learning assets delivered to customers increased from 20 to 35 per month, translating into a 15 percent increase in total learning solutions compared to the previous year, same time. If the team had started 2012 at this pace, DTCC Learning would be on target to deliver 180 percent more learning solutions than in 2011.

The feedback from both internal customers and DTCC Learning employees has also been glowing. One internal customer praised the "quick turnaround" and "quality of work," and another related that his post-Agile experience with DTCC Learning had been "nothing short of positive."

Even more encouraging were the personal team member acknowledgments. One DTCC Learning employee said, "I get excited to come to work every day." Another reported, "I can't believe how much work we're getting done."

Looking Ahead.

While we're encouraged by these early results, there have been a few bumps along the way. Each of the newly formed learning teams struggled with its own unique set of challenges, but the fact that DTCC Learning team members know and believe that they're empowered to solve these problems has created a level of engagement we never anticipated. The experience to date is best summed up by the words of one employee, "We can really make our own decisions."

Agile Revisited

In August 2012, I began a series of blog postings about the experiences of the DTCC Learning Group while implementing Agile as a development methodology for training programs. For those unfamiliar with the term, Agile is a software development technique that supports frequent releases of product features and functionality to customers. Agile accomplishes this by reducing the amount of administrative overhead typically associated with product development, instead focusing on human interactions more than tools and processes, delivering working software as opposed to product documentation, collaborating with customers versus relying on legal documentation, and responding nimbly to change, not a restricted, elaborate plan.

At DTCC, we saw firsthand that the changing nature of customer demands and expectations causing businesses to increase speed-to-market and more quickly respond to changing customer requirements was also applicable to training organizations that supported these businesses. So, like many software developers, we abandoned the waterfall approach to (learning) product development and adopted Agile instead.

The initial results of the Agile conversion were promising. In the first two months (post-Agile implementation) we saw a 75 percent increase in the number of learning assets that teams were able to deliver to customers monthly. In addition, the internal customers the team supported seemed to feel that the learning organization was now more responsive to their needs.

One business partner stated the following: "My experience in dealing with your team over the past month has been extremely positive . . . Your team was extremely helpful with their professionalism, quick turnaround on developing the SIMS, and the overall quality of work." Training employees also appeared to be more engaged. Several members of the training team stated they really felt empowered by the process.

While we were quite happy with the outcome, we wanted to be certain that the team wasn't just experiencing the "Hawthorne effect." In other words, we wanted to make sure that the team wasn't getting better simply because we were observing the results. After operating in the Agile mode for over nine months, we looked at the data again, this time comparing the organizational performance from Q1 2012 when we were using the waterfall approach, to Q1 2013, when we were operating totally in Agile.

The results were astounding. The number of learning assets delivered to customers in Q1 2013 as compared to the same period the previous year increased by 91 deliverables!

We realized some learning assets were naturally larger than others and, as a result, required more effort. We wanted to ensure we were looking at an apples-to-apples comparison, so we normalized the deliverable data by looking at what we called "work units"

(Agile calls these story points). We identified the smallest possible learning asset we could deliver as a single work unit, and sized the larger assets appropriately. An article was identified as requiring 1 work unit of effort, while developing a webinar might be 50 work units, and a product simulation, 30.

When we compared the number of work units delivered year to year, the results were even more dramatic. The work units of delivered learning assets increased almost ten times, from 394 work units of learning assets in Q1 2012 to 3,604 in Q1 2013. This meant we not only delivered more learning assets, but we were also able to deliver larger learning assets. Perhaps the most telling comparison of year-over-year performance arrived when we reviewed the types of learning assets the team was able to deliver.

In Q1 2012, the teams almost exclusively delivered articles or procedural documentation as learning assets to our customers. During the same period in 2013, the teams delivered a much more diverse set of learning solutions including webinars, webcasts, product simulations, and instructor-led training. The quantitative results from these year-to-year comparisons certainly indicate that the Agile approach for learning product does more than just work—it works well.

FINAL THOUGHTS

Businesses that have employed the Agile approach to product development have experienced increased customer satisfaction, highly engaged employees, greater visibility into the process of product releases, improved ability to address changes, and even higher quality products. Training organizations now finally have a template to help them realize the same benefits.

The changing nature of customer demands and expectations that have caused businesses to increase speed-to-market and more quickly respond to changing customer requirements make it imperative for learning teams to abandon the waterfall approach to (learning) product development and adopt Agile.

At DTCC this adoption resulted in a 75 percent increase in the number of learning assets that teams were able to deliver monthly to customers, an increase in the number of internal customers who felt that the learning organization was responsive to their needs more than ever, and a surge in employees who felt for the first time that, "We can really make our own decisions."